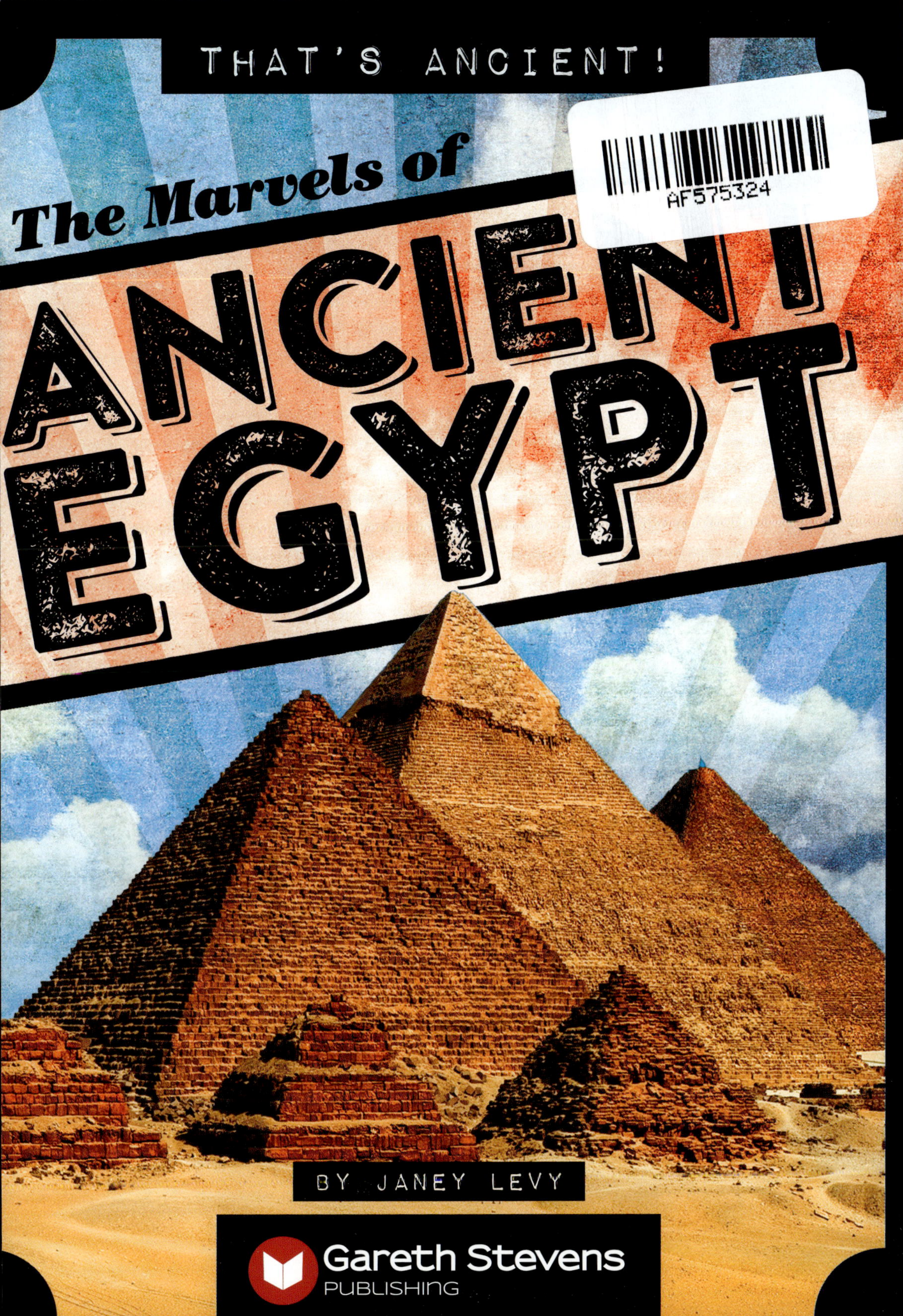

THAT'S ANCIENT!
The Marvels of
ANCIENT EGYPT
BY JANEY LEVY
Gareth Stevens
PUBLISHING

Please visit our website, www.garethstevens.com. For a free color catalog of all our high-quality books, call toll free 1-800-542-2595 or fax 1-877-542-2596.

Library of Congress Cataloging-in-Publication Data

Names: Levy, Janey, author. | Levy, Janey. That's ancient!
Title: The marvels of ancient Egypt / Janey Levy.
Description: New York : Gareth Stevens Publishing, 2022. | Series: That's ancient! | Includes bibliographical references and index.
Identifiers: LCCN 2020049189 (print) | LCCN 2020049190 (ebook) | ISBN 9781538265796 (library binding) | ISBN 9781538265772 (paperback) | ISBN 9781538265789 (set) | ISBN 9781538265802 (ebook)
Subjects: LCSH: Egypt—Civilization—To 332 B.C.—Juvenile literature.
Classification: LCC DT61 .L645 2022 (print) | LCC DT61 (ebook) | DDC 932/.01—dc23
LC record available at https://lccn.loc.gov/2020049189
LC ebook record available at https://lccn.loc.gov/2020049190

First Edition

Published in 2022 by
Gareth Stevens Publishing
29 E. 21st Street
New York, NY 10010

Designer: Katelyn E. Reynolds
Editor: Therese Shea

Photo credits: Cover, p. 1 WitR/Shutterstock.com; cover, pp. 1-32 (burst) Dawid Lech/Shutterstock .com; cover, pp. 1-32 (clouds) javarman/Shutterstock.com; p. 5 Peter Hermes Furian/Shutterstock .com; p. 7 Sophie McAulay/Shutterstock.com; p. 7 (inset) Gurgen Bakhshetyan/Shutterstock.com; pp. 8, 13 Cris Bouroncle/AFP via Getty Images; p. 9 Thomas Wyness/Shutterstock.com; p. 10 The Open University (http://www.open.ac.uk/cpdtasters/ga060/taster_hunting/hun_big_.jpg)/ Marcus Cyron/Wikipedia.org; p. 11 Vladimir Wrangel/Shutterstock.com; p. 13 (bottom) klyaksun/ Shutterstock.com; p. 14 Cyril Folliot/AFP via Getty Images; pp. 15, 25 Ethan Miller/Getty Images; p. 17 Mohamed Elshahed/AFP via Getty Images; p. 18 Marco Ossino/Shutterstock.com; p. 19 (top) Rogers Fund and Edward S. Harkness Gift, 1922/The Metropolitan Museum of Art; p. 19 (bottom) Rogers Fund, 1925/The Metropolitan Museum of Art; p. 20 Gift of Valdemar Hammer Jr., in memory of his father, 1936/The Metropolitan Museum of Art; p. 21 Rogers Fund, 1930/The Metropolitan Museum of Art; p. 21 (inset) NagyDodo/Shutterstock.com; p. 23 (left) ArchaiOptix/ Wikipedia.org; p. 23 (right) fotosullenuvole/Shutterstock.com; p. 24 Hayati Kayhan/Shutterstock .com; p. 25 (inset) Hulton Archive/Getty Images; p. 27 (inset) DEA/G. Dagli Orti/De Agostini via Getty Images; p. 27 Khaled Desouki/AFP via Getty Images; p. 29 (left) STR/AFP via Getty Images; p. 29 (right) nonneestudio/Shutterstock.com.

Printed in the United States of America

Some of the images in this book illustrate individuals who are models. The depictions do not imply actual situations or events.

CPSIA compliance information: Batch #CWGS22: For further information, contact Gareth Stevens, New York, New York, at 1-800-542-2595.

CONTENTS

Ancient Egypt....4

Pyramids and More....6

Mummies!....12

Write It Down....16

Feeding Everyone....20

Looking Good!....22

Tracking Time....26

And Still More....28

Glossary....30

For More Information....31

Index....32

Words in the glossary appear in **bold** type the first time they are used in the text.

Ancient

The history of Egypt stretches back thousands of years. Farming began there around 6000 BCE. The region's written history began between 3400 BCE and 3200 BCE. Ancient Egypt's great civilization—the time of the pharaohs—began around 3150 BCE.

What images spring to mind when you think of ancient Egypt? Perhaps you imagine the Pyramids of Giza, which are among ancient Egypt's most famous buildings. They're not Egypt's oldest pyramids, though. That honor belongs to the Step Pyramid of Djoser, or Zoser, which was built around 2670 BCE. It was the first monumental, or massive, stone building ever constructed anywhere!

But there's much more to ancient Egypt's accomplishments than its great buildings. Its achievements include a **hieroglyphic** writing system, papyrus sheets, and even toothpaste! Read on to learn more about ancient Egypt's amazing accomplishments.

THAT'S FASCINATING!

Upper Egypt and Lower Egypt were separate kingdoms until Upper Egypt conquered Lower Egypt around 3100 BCE, uniting the two kingdoms.

EGYPT'S TWO KINGDOMS

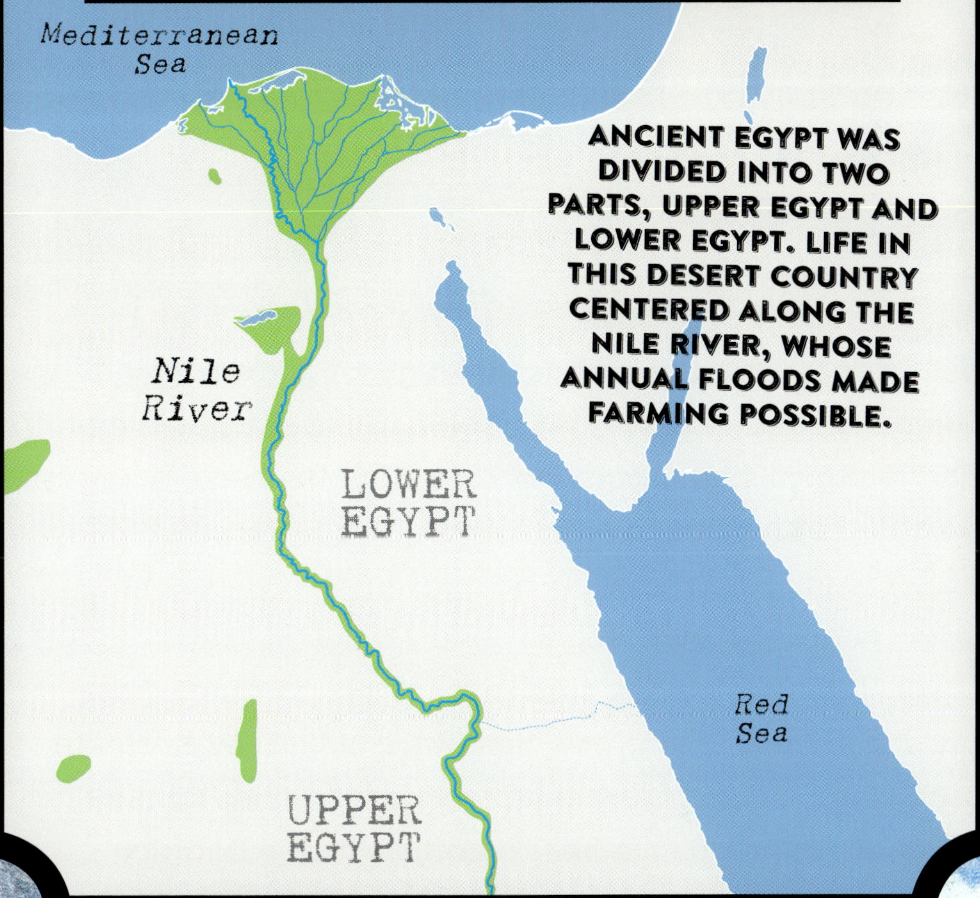

ANCIENT EGYPT WAS DIVIDED INTO TWO PARTS, UPPER EGYPT AND LOWER EGYPT. LIFE IN THIS DESERT COUNTRY CENTERED ALONG THE NILE RIVER, WHOSE ANNUAL FLOODS MADE FARMING POSSIBLE.

What's in a Name?

Ancient Egyptians called their country Kemet, which means "black land." That name referred to the dark, rich soil left behind by the Nile River after its annual floods. The name "Egypt" actually comes from the Greeks. They called the land Aegyptos, which was how they pronounced the name ancient Egyptians used for the city of Memphis: Hwt-Ka-Ptah. Memphis was important because it was the first capital of Egypt and was also a famous religious and trading center.

Pyramids AND MORE

Many people think first of the Pyramids of Giza when they imagine Egypt. These enormous pyramids were built as tombs for three pharaohs, or kings, of ancient Egypt. The oldest and largest—the Great Pyramid—was built by and for Khufu starting around 2550 BCE. The second largest belongs to Khufu's son Khafre and dates to around 2520 BCE. The third and smallest belongs to Menkaure and dates to around 2490 BCE.

The pyramids are such astonishing structures that experts still aren't sure how they were built. They're almost solid stone, but each contains a burial chamber for the pharaoh. It would have held a **coffin** with the pharaoh's mummy, as well as everything the pharaoh would need in the **afterlife**—including personal belongings, gold and silver treasures, and even food and drink!

THAT'S FASCINATING!

It's estimated that the Great Pyramid contains 2.3 million stone blocks. And those blocks weigh 2.5 to 15 tons (2.3 to 13.6 mt) *each*!

THE GREAT PYRAMID OF GIZA, SHOWN HERE, ORIGINALLY STOOD ABOUT 481 FEET (147 M) HIGH. FOR OVER 3,000 YEARS, IT WAS THE TALLEST MAN-MADE STRUCTURE IN THE WORLD!

Bent Pyramid

Not Quite a Pyramid

Ancient Egyptians didn't wake up one day, decide to build pyramids, and then build a perfect pyramid. Learning to build pyramids was a process. After the Step Pyramid of Djoser came the Bent Pyramid of Sneferu, built around 2600 BCE. It has sloping sides, like the Giza pyramids, but the slope changes partway up. The pyramid looks sort of bent, and this gave it its name. Many theories exist about why the slope changes, but nobody knows for sure.

Equal in fame to the pyramids is the nearby gigantic sculpture called the Great Sphinx, with a lion's body and a man's head wearing the royal Egyptian headdress. About 240 feet (73 m) long and 66 feet (20 m) tall, it was carved from a single block of limestone.

The Sphinx's origins are cloaked in mystery. It's directly lined up with Khafre's pyramid and its associated temples. Its face also resembles that of known statues of Khafre. So most experts believe Khafre built it. But some believe Khafre's brother or Khufu built it. Others claim the Sphinx is much, much older. Still others think the statue wasn't originally a Sphinx at all—they think it began as a statue of the jackal god Anubis and was later recarved!

TRACES OF PAINT SUGGEST THE GREAT SPHINX WAS ONCE COMPLETELY PAINTED IN BRIGHT COLORS.

THAT'S FASCINATING!

The only tools workers had for carving the Sphinx were stone hammers and copper **chisels**. Using those, it's been estimated it would have taken 100 workers about three years to complete the sculpture.

More Giant Sculptures

Ramses the Great ruled ancient Egypt for 66 years, from 1279 BCE to 1213 BCE. During his long reign, he built hundreds of buildings across Egypt. He also erected *enormous* statues of himself around the country. Some showed him standing; some showed him seated. He was displayed wearing the double crown of the pharaoh, called the pschent, representing both Upper and Lower Egypt. He was also shown wearing a false beard, or postiche, which was a sign of royalty.

Buildings and sculptures weren't the only art forms ancient Egyptians created. The walls of tombs were richly decorated with paintings or **low reliefs**. Common subjects were scenes of daily life, such as hunting, fishing, and harvesting crops. It's important to observe that these tombs were sealed after the dead were placed in them. The living would never see the images. So what purpose did they serve?

Tomb paintings and reliefs showed scenes from the dead person's life on Earth, to help the person's spirit, or life force, remember it. But the life force, or *ka*, needed something else as well. The *ka* needed food in the afterlife. Ancient Egyptians believed the magic of painting could turn represented scenes into reality. So those hunting, fishing, and crop scenes became food for the *ka*!

THIS TOMB PAINTING FROM ABOUT 1350 BCE SHOWS A COURT OFFICIAL NAMED NEBAMUN HUNTING BIRDS IN A MARSH. HIS WIFE STANDS BEHIND HIM, AND HIS DAUGHTER SITS BELOW HIM.

THAT'S FASCINATING!

Some of the hieroglyphs that accompany the painting of Nebamun say, "Rejoice, see the beauty in the place of the eternal repetition of the lifetimes!" This suggests that the painting represents, among other things, a perfect vision of the afterlife.

A Painted Lady

One of the most remarkable surviving pieces of ancient Egyptian art is the stunningly beautiful **bust** of Queen Nefertiti, created around 1340 BCE. It's not only in astonishingly good condition, it retains its original paint—giving modern viewers a rare glimpse of how Egyptian sculpture must have looked when new. This piece's good fortune may be due to the fact that it wasn't publicly displayed. It was discovered in a court sculptor's workshop and was a model for his assistants.

MUMMIES!

Ancient Egyptian mummies aren't the oldest purposely created mummies in the world. However, they're certainly the most famous. But the question is, *why* did they create these mummies?

Ancient Egyptians believed in an afterlife that required the physical body. Why? It has to do with ancient Egyptian notions of the soul and its relation to the body.

Ancient Egyptians believed the soul had many parts. Three were especially important for the afterlife: the *ka*, the *ba*, and the *akh*. The *akh* was the part of the soul that existed after death. It was formed by the union of the *ka* and the *ba* after death. But the *ka* would die if the body didn't exist. And without the *ka*, no *akh*. So the body had to be preserved.

THAT'S FASCINATING!

The word "mummy" comes from an Arabic word that refers to asphalt because it was once believed mummies were black because they'd been dipped in a type of asphalt. It's now known the black color results from oils, dirt, resins, and age.

PRESERVING THE BODY WAS SO IMPORTANT THAT TOMB WALLS FEATURED PRAYERS AND SPELLS MEANT TO PROTECT THE BODY.

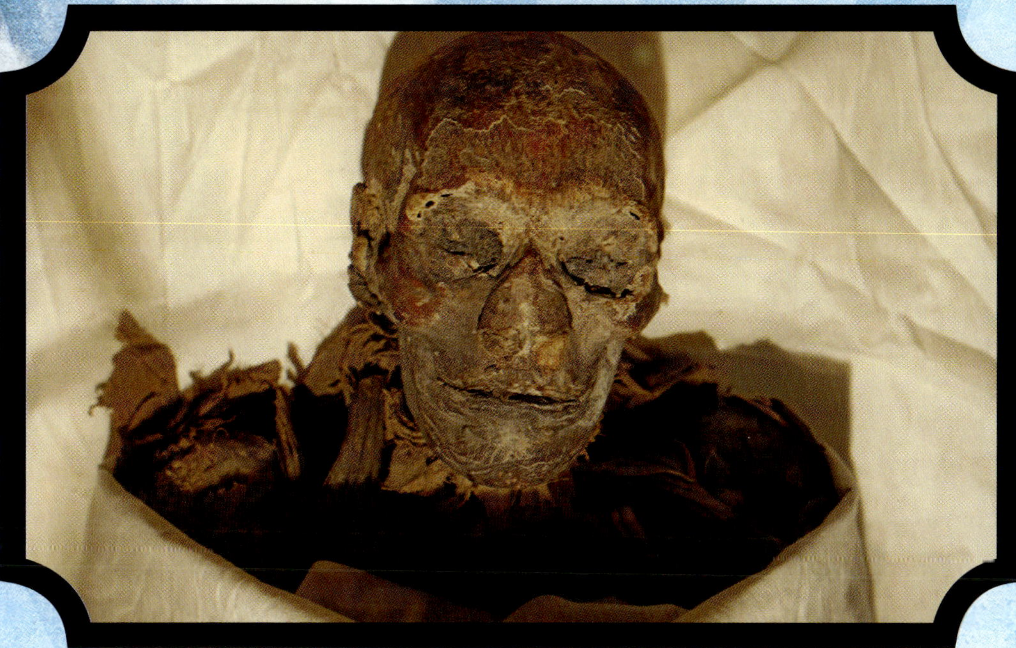

Making a Mummy

The first step in making a mummy was to stick a long hook up through the nose to pull out the brain. Then a cut was made along the body's left side, and the organs were removed. The heart was left, since it was believed to be the center of a person's being and intelligence. The body was then covered with a salt called natron for 40 days to remove all moisture. Finally, the body was wrapped in linen strips.

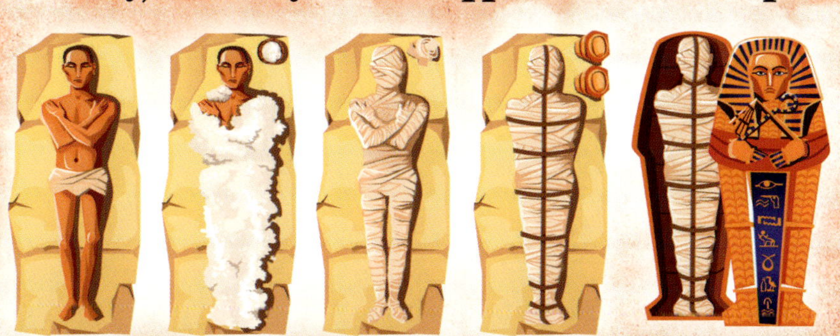

So what happened to the organs removed during the making of the mummy? They were preserved separately, and the stomach, liver, lungs, and intestines were put in special containers that are today called canopic jars.

Once the mummy was wrapped, it was placed in a **cartonnage** container. Then it was placed in a coffin and taken to the tomb along with the canopic jars. A funeral was held at the tomb, and priests performed the Opening of the Mouth ceremony. During the ceremony, a special instrument was used to touch the mouth, eyes, and other parts of the body to "open" them and restore their function. This prepared the dead person for the afterlife.

After the ceremony, the coffin and canopic jars were placed in the tomb and the tomb was sealed.

THESE ARE EXAMPLES OF CANOPIC JARS.

THAT'S FASCINATING!

Ancient Egyptians didn't bother to preserve the brain during the mummification process. They weren't sure what its function was, but they didn't think the dead would need it in the afterlife!

THIS IS A CANOPIC COFFIN. IT CONTAINED TUTANKHAMUN'S LIVER AND WAS PLACED IN A CANOPIC JAR.

Tutankhamun

Most ancient Egyptian tombs—including the Pyramids of Giza—were robbed in ancient times. But in 1922, a tomb was discovered that still contained its mummy and its treasures. That was the tomb of Tutankhamun. He died at the age of 19 in 1323 BCE after having been pharaoh for 10 years. Archaeologists were thrilled with the discovery. The tomb contained thousands of objects. Tutankhamun's mummy lay inside three coffins, one inside the other. The inside one was solid gold!

WRITE IT DOWN

How much have you written today? Maybe you used paper, a computer, or a smartphone. It's amazing that humans existed for thousands of years without writing. It wasn't until organized civilizations arose that writing appeared. Ancient Egypt created one of the world's first writing systems.

Egyptians invented hieroglyphs, a form of picture writing, around 3200 BCE. Over 1,000 hieroglyphs existed to begin with, although Egyptians reduced the number somewhat later. Some hieroglyphs represented an entire word, and some represented a sound.

No modern person could read hieroglyphs until the 1820s, when an ancient carved stone called the Rosetta Stone was translated. The stone had text in three languages, including Greek and hieroglyphs.

THAT'S FASCINATING!

Hieroglyph is the Greek name for Egyptian picture writing and means "holy writing." Ancient Egyptians called their writing "the gods' words" because they believed the gods invented writing.

THIS IS AN EXAMPLE OF EGYPTIAN HIEROGLYPHS, WHICH WERE COMMONLY CARVED ON MONUMENTS AND THE WALLS OF TOMBS.

More Than Hieroglyphs

Ancient Egyptians had other writing systems besides hieroglyphs. Because hieroglyphs had a somewhat elaborate pictorial form, they were difficult to write. So ancient Egyptians used them only on monuments. Around the same time hieroglyphs were invented, a simplified form of them was developed called hieratic. This form was used for government, business, literature, and religious **documents**. Around the 7th century BCE, an even simpler writing form called demotic replaced hieratic.

So what kind of surface were ancient Egyptians using to write documents on? They didn't have paper—it hadn't been invented yet. But around 3000 BCE, the Egyptians invented an excellent writing surface—papyrus.

Papyrus was made from the papyrus plant, which grew in shallow water in the Nile River **delta** and along the Nile River. Field workers harvested the plants, then transported them to processing centers. There, the stems were cut open, and the insides cut into strips to make papyrus sheets. The strips were laid down in two layers, at right angles to each other. Resin from the plant glued the layers together. The sheets were hammered flat, dried in the sun, and then polished with a piece of ivory or a shell.

THAT'S FASCINATING!

Sheets of papyrus weren't used to produce books like we have today. They were glued end to end to form scrolls that could be 100 feet (30 m) long or more!

PAPYRUS MAKES AN EXCELLENT SURFACE FOR BOTH WRITING AND PAINTING, AS CAN BE SEEN HERE. AND ALTHOUGH PAPYRUS ISN'T PAPER, BECAUSE IT DOESN'T MEET THE OFFICIAL DEFINITION OF PAPER, OUR WORD "PAPER" COMES FROM THE WORD "PAPYRUS."

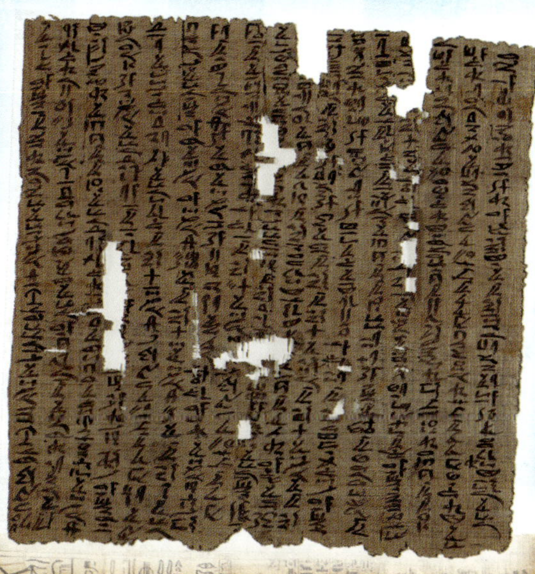

You Need More Than Papyrus to Write

Papyrus gave ancient Egyptians a wonderful writing surface. But it takes more than a writing surface to write. You need writing tools as well. That means ink, of course. And you need a means for applying the ink to the surface. Ancient Egyptians made black ink by combining vegetable gum, beeswax, and **soot**. Later, they replaced the soot with other natural materials to create colored inks. To apply the ink to the papyrus, they used brushes made from reeds.

Feeding EVERYONE

Ancient Egypt was a narrow strip of rich, dark soil along the Nile River surrounded by desert. That rich, dark soil was left behind after the Nile's annual floods. There, farmers raised crops to feed Egypt's entire population—possibly 1 to 1.5 million between 3000 BCE and 2000 BCE and perhaps as much as 3 million by 1000 BCE. How could Egyptians raise enough crops to feed everyone?

Ancient Egyptians invented tools that made farming easier and increased crop yield. One of those was a plow drawn by oxen, which was invented around 2500 BCE. This was a much faster and easier way to create the furrows, or grooves, for seeds than the old way—which had humans doing the work of pulling the plow or creating furrows with hoes.

THAT'S FASCINATING!

Plows were originally made entirely from wood — including the part that cut the furrows. It wasn't until later that the cutting part was made of metal.

THIS TOMB PAINTING SHOWS A MAN AND HIS WIFE IN THEIR FIELD. HE USES A PLOW PULLED BY OXEN TO PLOW THE FIELD. SHE WALKS BEHIND CARRYING A BASKET OF SEED AND TOSSING SEED INTO THE FURROWS PLOWED BY THE OXEN.

Crops Need Water

Even with the wet soil from the Nile floods, crops needed water. And ancient Egyptians needed to get water to crops distant from the Nile. So they created a system of irrigation canals with gates in them to control the water flow. Egyptians invented shadoofs to help get water from the Nile into the canals. These long poles had a bucket at one end and a weight at the other. The buckets were dipped into the Nile, then raised and emptied into the canals.

Looking GOOD!

Before you go out in the morning, do you brush your teeth, wash your face, and comb your hair? Most people do such things to clean up and look good. It might surprise you to learn ancient Egyptians were very concerned with looking good!

Ancient Egyptians are credited with inventing the practice of shaving. Men shaved not only their face but also their head. Even women and children shaved their head! This was both fashionable and a way to avoid the difficulties of keeping hair clean in the hot Egyptian climate. And it helped avoid lice. Eww!

However, it wasn't good to walk around bald in the blazing Egyptian sun. So people wore wigs. The wigs were made of real or artificial hair and were especially designed to keep the head cool.

THAT'S FASCINATING!

The importance of shaving gave rise to a whole new profession—the barber. Wealthy Egyptians were visited at home by barbers; ordinary people got their shaves outside under shade trees.

EGYPTIAN WOMEN'S WIGS WERE SOMETIMES ADORNED WITH BRAIDS, GOLD, AND IVORY. THE MORE ELABORATE THE WIG WAS, THE HIGHER THE SOCIAL RANK.

The Eyes Have It

In the pursuit of looking good, ancient Egyptians, men as well as women, applied eye makeup. They combined soot with the mineral galena to create a black substance called kohl. They could create green makeup by replacing soot with the mineral malachite. But fashion was only part of the reason Egyptians favored eye makeup. They believed it could cure eye diseases and protect them from curses!

What would looking good be without a nice smile? Getting that nice smile was hard for ancient Egyptians. Their bread had sand and dirt particles in it. (Remember, there was desert all around, plus the stones used to grind their grain added dirt particles.) The sand and dirt particles damaged their teeth. Unfortunately, ancient Egyptians didn't have dentists. Still, they did try to care for their teeth.

Ancient Egyptians had toothbrushes of a sort. They were the ragged ends of twigs. And they invented toothpaste! Their toothpaste probably won't sound very appealing to you, though. One recipe called for powdered ox hoofs, ashes, burnt eggshells, and **pumice**. Yuck! Another said to mix rock salt, mint, dried iris flower, and grains of pepper to create a "powder for white and perfect teeth."

THIS IS AN EXAMPLE OF AN EARLY TOOTHBRUSH.

THAT'S FASCINATING!

To help fight bad breath, ancient Egyptians invented breath mints! They were made of cinnamon, honey, and two fragrant tree resins called frankincense and myrrh.

Take a Look

How did ancient Egyptians know if their wig was on straight? How were they able to apply their eye makeup properly? They used mirrors! They didn't make the very first mirrors, but they invented metal handheld mirrors. They flattened sheets of metal such as copper, bronze, and silver, and then polished them until they were reflective. They added handles so the mirrors were easy to use and often decorated them. Both men and women used them.

THESE MIRROR CASES BELOW ARE SHAPED LIKE THE EGYPTIAN SYMBOL ANKH, WHICH REPRESENTED LIFE.

Tracking TIME

It's easy to find out the time today. You can check the nearest clock, or maybe you wear a watch or carry a phone that tells the time. But what did ancient Egyptians do thousands of years ago? They invented simple clocks to help them track time.

As early as 3500 BCE, Egyptians built tall, narrow structures called **obelisks**. They used these as **sundials** to tell time. They noted how the obelisk's shadow moved around it during the day. This allowed ancient Egyptians not only to tell time during the day but also to determine the longest and shortest days of the year.

By around 1500 BCE, Egyptians had invented sundials that were small and lightweight enough for people to carry with them.

THAT'S FASCINATING!

The part of a sundial that casts the shadow to indicate the time is called the gnomon (NOH-mahn). That name comes from a Greek word that means "to know."

BELOW IS AN ANCIENT EGYPTIAN OBELISK, STILL STANDING, ALONG WITH TWO KINDS OF SUNDIALS.

Telling Time in the Dark

One obvious problem with sundials is that they require sunlight to work. If it's night or a dark cloudy day, sundials can't tell you the time. Ancient Egyptians solved that problem with the water clock. This was a stone container with a tiny hole in the bottom. Water dripped through the hole at a steady rate into a container below. Hours were measured by marks on the container receiving the water.

And STILL MORE

The creations you've read about here are just some of the ancient Egyptians' many innovations. But that's not all.

Did you drink milk or juice from a glass this morning? You can thank the ancient Egyptians. Egyptians, along with Mesopotamians, invented glass and made the first glass vessels.

Do you lock your door at night or when you leave in the morning? Thank Egyptians again. They invented mechanical locks.

Do you enjoy bowling? Ancient Egyptians invented that too, although their game was different from the modern one. They weren't trying to knock down pins; they were trying to roll their ball into a hole and knock their opponent's ball out of the way. You might be surprised to discover how many more parts of modern daily life owe their origin to the ancient Egyptians!

THAT'S FASCINATING!

Ancient Egyptians also invented police. Police used dogs and even monkeys to help capture criminals. Criminals could be punished with beatings or by having their ears or nose cut off!

MORE EGYPTIAN INNOVATIONS

Egyptian glass

GLASS (3500 BCE)

DOOR LOCK (4000 BCE)

POLICE (AROUND 2200 BCE)

PERFUME (4000 BCE)

BOWLING (2ND TO 3RD CENTURY CE)

bowling ball and pins

What a Lovely Smell!

Ancient Egyptians also created *kyphi*, which is considered one of the first perfumes in the world. It was an expensive perfume whose ingredients—including frankincense, myrrh, pine resin, cinnamon, and mint—had to be imported. Less expensive perfumes were made from roots, herbs, and flowers such as honeysuckle, iris, and jasmine. These were ground into a paste, then mixed with oil or fat. As with eye makeup, both men and women wore perfume.

GLOSSARY

afterlife: an existence after death

bust: a sculpture that consists of just the head and shoulders of a person

cartonnage: material made of many thicknesses of linen or papyrus glued together and usually coated with stucco

chisel: a metal tool with a straight, flat end used for cutting and shaping wood or stone

coffin: a box for burying a dead person

delta: land shaped like a triangle at the mouth of a river

document: a formal piece of writing

hieroglyphic: having to do with written characters that look like pictures

low relief: a kind of sculpture in which the carved forms stick out slightly above the surface

obelisk: a column of stone with a square base, sides that slope in, and a pyramid on top

pumice: very lightweight, gray volcanic stone

soot: the black powder formed when something is burned

sundial: a device that uses the sun to show the time of day and that consists of a surface with line markings and a raised object that casts a shadow onto the surface

FOR MORE INFORMATION

BOOKS

Honovich, Nancy. *1,000 Facts About Ancient Egypt*. Washington, DC: National Geographic, 2019.

McDonald, Angela. *Ancient Egypt*. New York, NY: DK Publishing, 2017.

Moroney, Morgan E. *Gods and Goddesses of Ancient Egypt: Egyptian Mythology for Kids*. Emeryville, CA: Rockridge Press, 2020.

WEBSITES

Ancient Egypt
www.ancientegypt.co.uk/menu.html
Check out this interactive website from the British Museum.

Ancient Egyptian Civilization
www.khanacademy.org/humanities/world-history/world-history-beginnings/ancient-egypt-hittites/a/egypt-article
Discover more about ancient Egypt.

Explore Ancient Egypt
www.pbs.org/wgbh/nova/ancient/explore-ancient-egypt.html
Go inside the Great Pyramid, walk around the Sphinx, and explore other ancient Egyptian monuments.

INDEX

afterlife 6, 10, 12, 14
Bent Pyramid of Sneferu 7
bowling 28, 29
canopic jars 14
eye makeup 23, 25, 29
farming 4, 5, 20, 21
glass 28, 29
Great Sphinx 8, 9
hieroglyphs 4, 10, 16, 17
irrigation canals 21
Lower Egypt 4, 5, 9
low reliefs 10
mechanical locks 28, 29
mirrors 25
mummies 6, 12, 13, 14, 15
Nile River 5, 18, 20, 21
Opening of the Mouth ceremony 14
papyrus 4, 18, 19
perfume 29
police 28, 29
pyramids 4, 6, 7, 8, 15
Pyramids of Giza 4, 6, 7, 15
Ramses the Great 9
Rosetta Stone 16
shaving 22
Step Pyramid of Djoser 4, 7
sundials 26, 27
tomb paintings 10, 21
toothbrushes/toothpaste 4, 24
Tutankhamun 15
Upper Egypt 4, 5, 9
water clock 27
wigs 22, 23, 25
writing systems 4, 16, 17